All About Britain

Julie Hart

Burlington Books

All About Britain

Julie Hart

Burlington Books
P. O. Box 54411
3721 Limassol
Cyprus
Burlington Books is an imprint of Danos Books Ltd.

The publisher gratefully acknowledges the following for providing photographs:
Alamy / Chris Gomersall: page 9 (Iona Island); Alamy / Neil Tingle: page 33 (Rafael Nadal); Alamy / Philippe Hays: pages 11 & 15 (beefeater); ASAP / Alamy: cover (Queen's guard), 38 & 41 (Elizabeth I); ASAP / Rex Features: pages 13, 15 (judge), 22 (Prince Andrew, Prince Edward, Prince Harry & Prince William), 23, 24, 41 (J.K. Rowling) , 47 (Jamie Oliver); Corel Corp.: page 6 (Glamis Castle); Everett Collection: cover & pages 37 (Harry Potter), 47 (Mr Bean); Image Bank / Getty Images: pages 6, 39 & 41 (The Beatles); Jorvik Viking Centre, York: page 18; Mary Evans Picture Library: Pages 38 & 41 (Sir Winston Churchill); Photos.com / Jupiter Images: pages 6 (Viking helmet), 41 (Charles Dickens); Shutterstock, Inc.: Cover (Union Jack, Stonehenge), pages 6 (map, loch ness monster, canal boat, Big Ben, Stonehenge), 8, 9 (ghost), 10, 11 (Tower of London), 12 (bagpipes), 14, 15 (Queen's guard), 17, 19-21, 22 (Queen Elizabeth II, Prince Charles), 26, 27 (Christmas tree), 28 (Christmas decoration), 31, 32, 34, 36 (stage), 44, 46, 56; Thomson Reuters: pages 22 (Princess Anne), 33 (Wimbledon Stadium).

The publisher would like to thank the following people:

Castellano:	Alicia Ruiz Cuéllar
Català:	Maria Esteve Serraviñals
Euskara:	Edurne Azkue Urrestilla
Galego:	Ramón Nicolás Rodríguez

ISBN 978-9963-48-548-2

Burlington Reader No. NE1.08

10 9 8 7 6 5 4 3 2 1
20 19 18 17 16 15 14 13 12 11

CONTENTS

Introducción

All About Britain te lleva de viaje por Gran Bretaña, una tierra con una diversidad cultural extraordinaria y una fascinante colección de sitios míticos y de interés histórico. Gran Bretaña es un lugar de intriga y leyendas, donde nació mucha gente famosa e influyente. El libro contiene información sobre algunas de sus conocidas atracciones, ceremonias, tradiciones y celebridades del país, así como muchos datos curiosos y poco conocidos. Descubrirás por qué hay fantasmas en el castillo escocés de Glamis, por qué hay cuervos en la Torre de Londres, por qué los jueces británicos llevan peluca y mucho, mucho más. Así que empieza con el Capítulo 1 y conócelo todo sobre Gran Bretaña. ¡Disfruta del viaje!

Introducció

All About Britain et porta de viatge per la Gran Bretanya, una terra amb una diversitat cultural extraordinària i una fascinant col·lecció de llocs mítics i d'interès històric. La Gran Bretanya és un lloc d'intriga i de llegendes on va néixer molta gent famosa i influent. El llibre conté informació sobre algunes de les seves conegudes atraccions, cerimònies, tradicions i celebritats del país, així com moltes dades curioses i poc conegudes. Descobriràs per què hi ha fantasmes al castell escocès de Glamis, per què hi ha corbs a la Torre de Londres, per què els jutges britànics porten perruca i molt, molt més. Així que comença amb el Capítol 1 i coneix-ho tot sobre la Gran Bretanya. Gaudeix del viatge!

Sarrera

All About Britain liburuak Britainia Handian barrena eramango zaitu. Kultur aniztasun handiko lurraldea izanik, txoko mitiko eta historiko interesgarriz josita dago Britainia Handia. Intriga eta legenden herrialde hau jende ospetsu eta itzal handiko askoren sorterri ere bada. Liburu honek ezagunak ditugun hainbat ikuskizun, erritu, ohitura eta pertsonen berri emango dizu, batetik, eta informazio bitxi eta ez hain ezagun ugari, bestetik. Eskoziako Glamis gazteluan mamuak zergatik dauden jakingo duzu, zergatik beleak Londresko Dorrean, zergatik daramatzaten ileordeak epaile britainiarrek, eta askoz kontu gehiago. Hasi berehala 1. kapituluarekin eta ikasi Britainia Handiaz ikasteko dagoen guztia. Gozatu bidaiaz!

Limiar

All About Britain lévate de viaxe por Gran Bretaña, unha terra cunha diversidade cultural extraordinaria e unha apaixonante colección de sitios míticos e de interese histórico. Gran Bretaña é un lugar de intriga e lendas, onde naceu moita xente famosa e influente. O libro contén información sobre algunhas das súas coñecidas atraccións, cerimonias, tradicións e persoeiros do país, así como moitos datos curiosos e pouco coñecidos. Descubrirás por que hai pantasmas no castelo escocés de Glamis, por que hai corvos na Torre de Londres, por que os xuíces británicos levan perruca e moito, moito máis. De maneira que comeza co Capítulo 1 e coñéceo todo sobre Gran Bretaña. Goza da viaxe!

MAP OF BRITAIN

PRE-READING ACTIVITIES

1 Label the picture with the words below.

castle flag lake clock queen bell

2 Write the words in the correct category.

husband egg son guard beans Scotland
Wales soldier judge wife sausage England

Jobs	Places in Britain	Food	Family

CHAPTER 1

Ghost Tour of Britain

SPOOKY TOURS

Day 1 Our tour starts at the Tower of London, the home of some very famous ghosts. Many years ago, the Tower of London was a prison. Henry VIII's second wife, Anne Boleyn, died here and people sometimes see her ghost! The "princes in the tower", Edward V of England and his brother Prince Richard, were also in prison here and people see their ghosts, too. Some believe their uncle, Richard III, killed them because he wanted to be king.

Next, we travel to Covent Garden Underground Station – the only train station with a ghost! An actor called William Terriss died there in 1897 and his ghost visits quite often!

Day 2 We leave London and travel north to Scotland. Our first stop in Scotland is Glamis Castle, one of Britain's oldest castles. The Earl of Strathmore and his family live there with a lot of ghosts. One of them is "the Grey Lady", the ghost of Lady Janet Douglas. In 1537, the authorities accused her of trying to **poison** King James V and **burned her at the stake**. People say her ghost is very sad and quiet.

We spend the night in Scotland, at the Castle of Park. This very old castle is now a hotel. In the corridors, people sometimes see the ghost of a mysterious Green Lady. Many believe she was a servant at the castle and her employers **dismissed** her because she was **pregnant**. She later committed suicide.

Glamis Castle

Boat Visiting Iona Island

Day 3 In the morning, we travel by boat to Iona, a beautiful island next to Scotland. In 794, Vikings came here to look for treasure. They killed the monks in Iona Abbey and escaped with all the treasures from it. According to people on the island, Viking ghosts sometimes visit them today. They arrive on Viking ships and return to the abbey. Look for them there!

Day 4 After the boat tour, we say goodbye to Scotland and travel south to Wales.

In Wales, we go on a fascinating boat tour along Montgomery Canal to **search for** the ghost of a Welsh princess called Eira. Princess Eira **fell in love with** a common man and wanted to marry him. This was against the law, so somebody killed her and **buried** her body next to the canal.

CHAPTER 2

British Jobs and Uniforms

Queen's Guards

This is a Queen's Guard at Buckingham Palace. His job is to protect the Queen of England. His hat is from **bearskin** and it's very heavy. Queen Elizabeth is at home today, so the flag is flying on the roof and there are four guards in front of the palace. When the Queen isn't here, there is no flag and there are only two guards.

It isn't easy to be a Queen's Guard because they mustn't move. But every ten minutes, they can walk up and down in front of the **sentry box**. Visitors often talk to them and ask them questions, but they mustn't answer. At half past eleven every morning, new guards arrive and they change. The visitors love watching the "Changing of the Guard" ceremony.

Beefeaters

This is Moira Cameron and she guards the Tower of London. She's the first female beefeater in history. Why do people call her this strange name? In the old days, there weren't many cows in Britain, so only the royal family and the Tower guards ate **beef**. People called the guards "beefeaters" because of this. The birds at the Tower ate beef, too. There are hundreds of black birds at the Tower of London today. The birds are **ravens**. Every day, a beefeater gives the ravens some meat to keep them at the Tower. According to legend, the ravens protect the kings and queens of England, so the ravens must never leave the Tower.

Bagpipe Players

This man is a bagpipe player. He stands at a tourist site in the Scottish Highlands and plays for the tourists. They love his music and his clothes. He wears a kilt – a special skirt with a tartan design. Each Scottish clan has got a different type of tartan. They also wear white socks with a pattern of the same colours as the kilt. Bagpipe players sometimes play Scottish dance music at weddings, parties and festivals. They can also play sad, solemn music at funerals and official ceremonies.

Judges

This woman is a judge. Judges have got very important, responsible jobs, and they wear a special uniform – a long black robe and a white wig.

Three hundred years ago, many important people covered their hair with these wigs. But today, only British judges must wear the wigs – and it's a very old tradition. The tradition started because many criminals wanted to hurt judges. They were responsible for sending the criminals to prison. The wigs and robes hide the judges' hair and bodies, so it is more difficult to recognise them outside the courtroom.

CHAPTERS 1-2 ACTIVITIES

1 Use the words in the puzzle to complete the sentences below. Then circle the answers in the puzzle and follow the route to help the ghost get to the castle.

1. The British .... is red, white and blue.
2. A house has got a .... on it.
3. This shirt is very .... I can't buy it.
4. I love to .... to this music.
5. The young girl is .... She is crying.
6. A .... eats grass in a field.
7. The Queen's mother was over 100 years old when she ....
8. My mother's brother is my ....

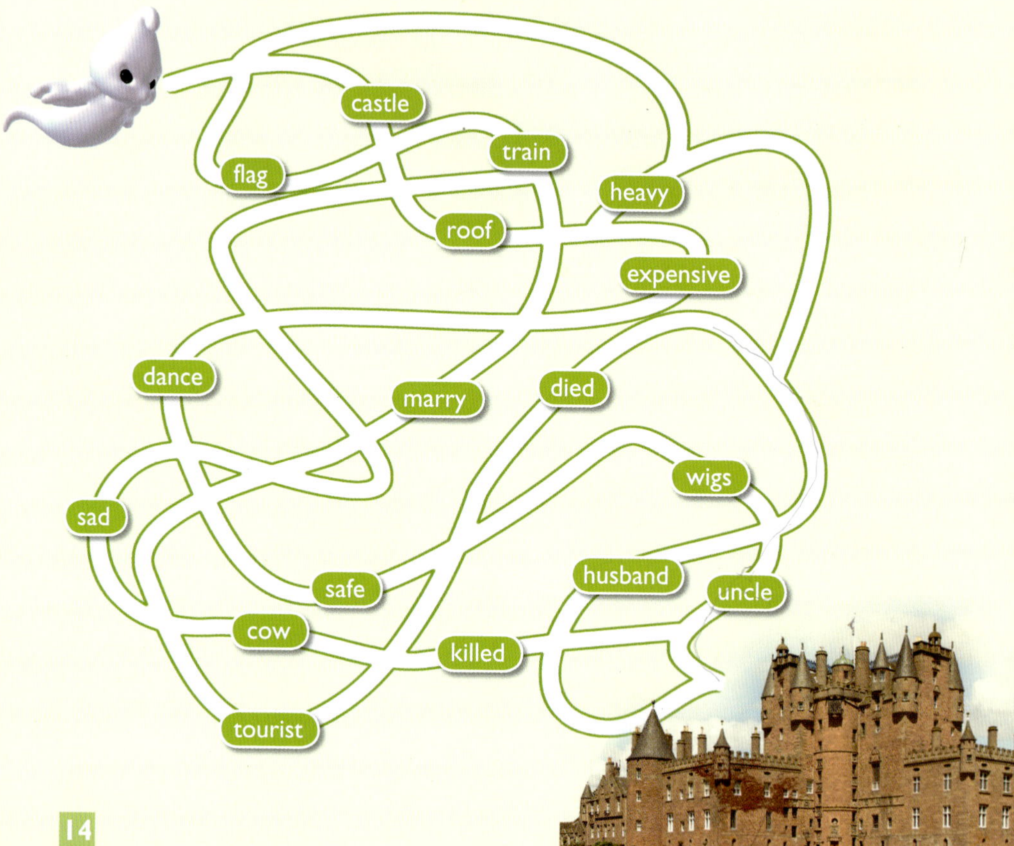

2 Who is speaking? Match each ghost to the correct speech bubble.

a. A Viking ghost *b. Princess Eira* *c. Lady Janet Douglas*
d. Prince Edward *e. Anne Boleyn*

1 c *I live in Glamis Castle.*

2 a *I kill people for their treasures.*

3 d *My uncle wanted to be king.*

4 e *I was King Henry VIII's wife.*

5 b *I love that man but I can't marry him.*

3 Who is it? Match the characters to the questions below.

1 *Beefeater*

2 *Queen's guard*

3 *Judge*

4 *Bagpipe player*

Who …

.... a. mustn't move?
.... b. guards the Tower of London?
.... c. wears a tartan skirt?
.... d. wears a white wig?
.... e. sends criminals to prison?
.... f. sometimes works at weddings?
.... g. wears a hat from bearskin?
.... h. gives meat to birds?

Did You know?

The beefeaters guard the Crown Jewels at the Tower of London. Once, these very expensive objects were in Westminster Abbey, but people often tried to steal them. Nobody can steal them now!

CHAPTER 3

Famous Sites

Big Ben

Everyone thinks Big Ben is the name of a famous London clock, but actually it's the name of the big bell inside the clock tower. You can hear the bell every hour. The clock is on a tall tower on the Houses of Parliament. It is over 150 years old, but it still works very well. There are thousands of old British coins on the clock's pendulum. The coins are very heavy and they hold the pendulum in the correct position.

During meetings of Parliament, a light shines above the clock so the people of London always know about the meetings. They can go into the visitors' gallery and listen, too. At night, lights illuminate the tower and it looks fantastic.

Stonehenge

At Stonehenge, on Salisbury Plain in South-West England, there is a mysterious ring of stones. The ring is about 4,000 years old. There is one entrance to the ring, and there are more stones in the centre. These enormous stones aren't from the area. People carried them for nearly 400 kilometres from the mountains of Wales! How did they do this very difficult task? Nobody knows!

The position of the stones is very interesting. They correspond to the position of the sun and the moon at different times of the year. In ancient times, people believed that the sun and moon had magic powers. So they probably used the stones for magic ceremonies or to **make wishes**.

CHAPTER 4

Attractions

Jorvik Museum, York

Come and meet Vikings at the Jorvik Museum in York! One thousand years ago, Vikings lived in Britain. Jorvik, now York, was their capital city. Archeologists discovered ruins of Viking buildings and walls under the ground. You can see the ruins at the museum and ride under the ground through a Viking village. There are models of the Vikings and their animals. The Vikings talk and the children play games. They look real! You can smell the village too, so be careful when you pass the Viking toilets! After the ride, you can look at the Viking **tools** and **pots** in the museum and you can stamp your name in the Viking alphabet. It's a fun place to visit.

Hadrian's Wall

Experience the great Roman Wall in the North of England. Two thousand years ago, Hadrian's Wall was 117 kilometres long, across all of England! But why was it there?

People in Scotland didn't want Romans in Britain, so the Scots often entered England to fight the Romans. The Roman emperor, Hadrian, built a long wall across the north of England. Roman soldiers stood on the wall and guarded. This stopped the Scots for many years. There were 16 forts and 18 castles along the wall. Today, you can see some ruins of the wall and the forts.

CHAPTERS 3-4 ACTIVITIES

1 Complete the puzzle.

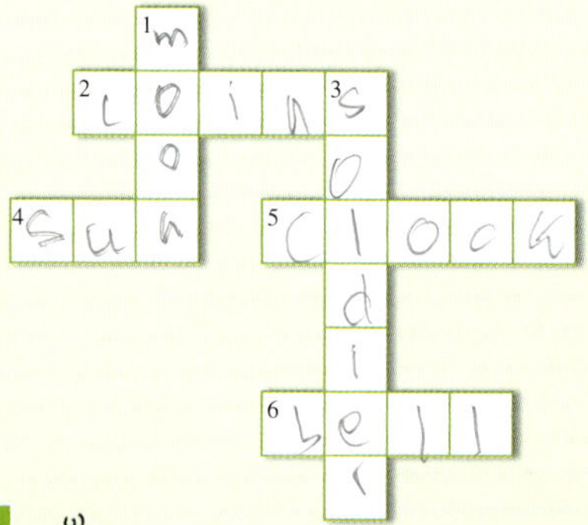

Across ➤

2

4

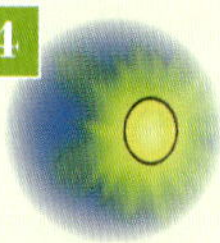

5

6

Down ▼

1

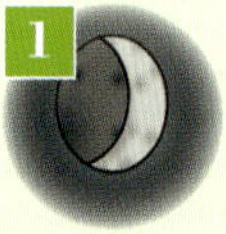

3

2 Complete the sentences. Make words from the letters on the stones to find the answers. The first letter is always at the top.

1. It's raining. Let's stay ....
2. Please listen.................... to me. I'm talking to you.
3. Our teacher isn't in the classroom because she's in a meeting.................... .
4. I can't carry.................... these books. They're heavy.
5. He lives in a small village.................... .

3 Match A and B to make sentences.

A		B
1. There are a lot of British coins	....	a. at the Jorvik Museum.
2. The Stonehenge site is	....	b. from entering England.
3. You can ride under the ground	....	c. in the North of England.
4. You can see Roman ruins	....	d. in South-West England.
5. Hadrian's wall prevented the Scots	....	e. in Big Ben.

4 Play noughts and crosses. Put X on the false sentences and put O on the true sentences. You must get three Xs in a row.

1. Big Ben is the name of a famous clock.
2. You can hear Big Ben once a day.
3. Visitors can go into the Houses of Parliament.
4. The ring at Stonehenge is 150 years old.
5. The stones at Stonehenge come from Scotland.
6. There are Viking toilets at the Jorvik Museum.
7. In York, you can make your name from the Viking alphabet.
8. Roman soldiers stood on Hadrian's Wall.
9. Hadrian's Wall was across all of Scotland.

Did You know?

Most visitors to London want to visit Big Ben. But today, many visitors are disappointed because they can only see Big Ben from the outside. For security reasons, only residents of the UK can go inside the tower of Big Ben. But there isn't a lift, so visitors must go up 334 stairs to reach the top!

CHAPTER 5

Royal Ceremonies and Traditions

The Royal Family

Elizabeth II is the Queen of England, Scotland, Wales and Northern Ireland. She and her husband, the Duke of Edinburgh, usually live at Buckingham Palace. The Queen's son, Charles, is the successor to the throne. His two sons are William and Harry. Charles has also got two brothers, Andrew and Edward, and a sister, Anne.

Prince Charles

Princess Anne

Prince Andrew

Prince Edward

Prince Harry & Prince William

The Royal Wedding

Everybody loves royal weddings! In April 2011, millions of people all over the world watched the wedding of Prince William and Kate Middleton. It was a spectacular occasion. The wedding cake was very special. It had the four national flowers of the UK: the rose (England), the **thistle** (Scotland), the **shamrock** (Northern Ireland) and the **daffodil** (Wales).

Prince William first **noticed** Kate at a university **fashion show** in 2001. They were both students of art history at St Andrews University, Scotland. Kate was one of the models at the show and William wanted to meet her. They dated for eight years and finally, William asked her to be his wife.

Prince William's full name is William Arthur Philip Louis Mountbatten-Windsor. William's life was not always easy. His parents divorced when he was eight years old. He was very **close** to his mother, Diana, Princess of Wales. Then, she died in a car accident when he was 15 years old. William has got a lot of responsibility because he is the successor to the throne after his father, Prince Charles. But now he's got a wife to help him!

The State Opening of Parliament

Before a new government starts, there is a special ceremony for the opening of Parliament. The Queen reads a **speech** to all the ministers at the Houses of Parliament. Before the ceremony, a guard searches with a candle for **gunpowder** in the **cellars**. This tradition started in 1605 because a man, Guy Fawkes, tried to assassinate the King in the Parliament building.

Ceremony of the Keys

The Ceremony of the Keys is a 700-year-old English tradition. It takes place at the Tower of London at 21:53 every night. The chief beefeater **locks** all the gates with keys. A guard stops him and asks him a question. Then, they return the keys to a special room.

Maundy Thursday

Maundy Thursday is the beginning of the three-day celebration of Easter. On that day, the Queen gives money to a group of old people. This tradition is over 1,000 years old. In the past, the king or queen washed the feet of the poor in Westminster Abbey on Maundy Thursday.

The Queen's Birthday Card

The Queen sends a birthday card to people on their 100th birthday. She signs it Elizabeth R.

The card says: *"I am pleased to hear that you are celebrating your 100th birthday. I send my congratulations and best wishes to you on this very special day. Elizabeth R".*

CHAPTER 6

Holidays and Festivals

October
31

Halloween

Halloween is on 31st October. According to legend, ghosts, witches and fairies are especially active on this night. To celebrate, people wear frightening costumes and tell ghost stories. Children use pumpkins to make lanterns with horrible faces and they put candles inside. Then they go to their neighbours' homes and say, "Trick or treat". The neighbours must give them a treat, or the children **play a trick on** them.

Guy Fawkes

November
5

"Remember, remember the 5th of November!"

On 5th November, people remember Guy Fawkes and his terrible plan to assassinate the King in the Houses of Parliament. So on this day, people make Guys from old clothes, and put them on a bonfire. They also celebrate with **fireworks**.

Christmas

At Christmas, people put trees in their homes and decorate them with lights. In the story of Jesus, the Three Kings brought presents to baby Jesus. Because of this, people give presents at Christmas and usually put them under the Christmas tree. On Christmas Day, people eat a special meal with turkey.

April Fool's Day

On 1st April, people in Britain trick their friends. Reporters also invent false news reports on this day. Some of the reports are very funny, but people often believe them!

The first April Fool's news report was in 1957. The news programme showed people in Switzerland picking spaghetti from plants. According to the report, spaghetti plants were strong and tall that year because of the warm weather. Hundreds of people phoned the television station. They wanted to buy the spaghetti plants for their garden! April Fools!

CHAPTERS 5-6 ACTIVITIES

1 Complete the words and phrases in the sentences.

1. We've got nice n _ i _ h _ o _ r _ on our street.
2. People usually have a celebration on their b _ r _ h _ a _.
3. Kim's father is her mother's h _ s _ a _ d.
4. C _ n _ r _ t _ l _ t _ o _ s! You got 100 in your exam!
5. John's family haven't got any money. They're very p _ o _.
6. The w _ a _ h _ r in England is cold and rainy in the winter.

2 Match the pictures to the words.

.... a. turkey
.... b. gate
.... c. present
.... d. candle
.... e. key
.... f. witch

3 Match A and B to make sentences.

A		B
1. The Ceremony of the Keys	....	a. wear costumes and say "Trick or treat".
2. On Maundy Thursday, the Queen	....	b. decorate their homes with lights.
3. On a person's 100th birthday, the Queen	....	c. takes place at 21:53 every night.
4. On Halloween, people	....	d. remember Guy Fawkes.
5. On Bonfire Night, people	....	e. gives money to old people.
6. At Christmas, people	....	f. invent false news reports.
7. On April Fool's Day, reporters	....	g. sends a birthday card.

4 Choose the correct answer.

1. The Duke of Edinburgh is the Queen's **son** / **uncle** / **husband**.
2. The Queen of England has got **two** / **three** / **four** children.
3. Once a year, the king or queen washed people's **feet** / **houses** / **clothes**.
4. People tell frightening stories on **April Fool's Day** / **Halloween** / **Maundy Thursday**.
5. At Christmas, people put presents under a **spaghetti plant** / **tree** / **lantern**.
6. You can't believe your friends on **April Fool's Day** / **Bonfire Night** / **Christmas Day**.

Did You know?

Every Christmas, at 3 o'clock in the afternoon, the Queen gives her Christmas message to the people of the UK. People can watch her on TV or listen to her on the radio. George V, the Queen's grandfather, started this tradition with his first Christmas radio message in 1932.

CHAPTER 7

Food

Breakfast

An American tourist is staying at a hotel in York. He's ordering breakfast.

Waiter: Good morning. Can I take your order now?

Tourist: Yes, please. What do you recommend for breakfast today?

Waiter: You can have a traditional English breakfast with eggs, sausages, black pudding and beans.

Tourist: Black pudding? What's that?

Waiter: It's **dried blood**. It's delicious!

Tourist: *Blood!* No, thanks – I'm not a vampire! Can I have the eggs, sausages and beans, please?

Waiter: Do you want a nice cup of English tea with milk?

Tourist: Milk? Who drinks tea with milk?

Waiter: Oh, the English love their tea with milk!

Lunch

Now, the tourist is ordering lunch in a café. There's a traditional British menu.

Afternoon Tea

It's four o'clock in the afternoon. The tourist is having "afternoon tea" with sandwiches and scones. The scones are delicious! They aren't very sweet, but they've got cream and jam on them. The tourist is drinking English tea with milk!

CHAPTER 8

Sport

Football, cricket and tennis are national sports in Britain. Here's some information about them.

Football

The English invented the modern **rules** of football. Sheffield Football Club was the first football club in the world and it started in 1857. The English FA Cup was the first national competition. England has got 40,000 football clubs, so football is very important to the English!

Cricket

You play cricket with a small, hard ball and a long bat. Here are the rules:

- There are two teams, with eleven players in each team.
- The first half of the game is the "first **innings**". One team throws the ball and the other team hits it with the bat. The batsmen must wear **leg guards**, gloves and a **helmet** for protection. They hit the ball, and then they must run between two **wickets**. This is a *run*.
- In the second innings, the teams change roles.
- The team with more *runs* wins the game.

Tennis

Wimbledon was the first tennis **tournament** in the world. The tournament is once a year in June and July. It's the dream of every tennis player to win Wimbledon. The winner is very famous and gets millions of pounds in prize money.

Members of the royal family always go to the tournaments and it's a tradition for people to eat strawberries and cream between the games. The Millennium Building at Wimbledon has got **facilities** for the players, reporters and club members. There's also a new **court** with 2,000 seats and a roof to protect the players from the rain.

CHAPTERS 7-8 ACTIVITIES

1 Read the clues and follow the path of the ball. Who scores the goal? Choose the correct answer.

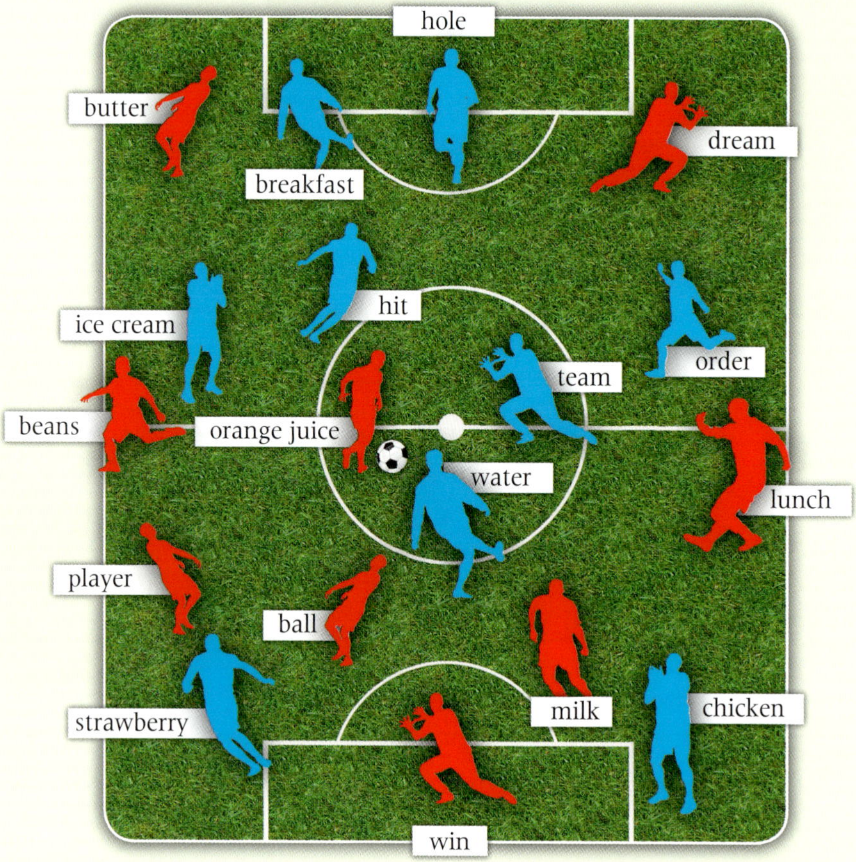

Clues

1. a fruit drink
2. a cold and sweet dessert
3. the first meal of the day
4. a group of players
5. ask for food in a restaurant
6. the second meal of the day
7. a round item for sport
8. a white drink
9. a small red fruit
10. to be victorious

The **red** / **blue** team scores the goal.

2 Tick (✓) the sentences true (T) or false (F).

	T	F
1. A traditional English breakfast includes eggs and sausages.	☐	☐
2. The English people usually drink coffee in the morning.	☐	☐
3. Shepherd's pie has got fish and peas in it.	☐	☐
4. Toad in the hole has got sausages and Yorkshire pudding.	☐	☐
5. People have sandwiches and scones for afternoon tea.	☐	☐
6. Scones are very sweet.	☐	☐

3 Tick (✓) the correct sport.

	Football	Cricket	Tennis
1. England had the first national competition.			
2. The modern rules are from England.			
3. There are special games in June and July.			
4. The team with more runs wins the game.			
5. People eat strawberries and cream at the tournaments.			
6. The players wear special protection.			

Did you know?

Nettie Honeyball started the first British Women's Football Club in 1894. About thirty women trained twice a week at a park in Hornsey in north London. Today, there are over 150,000 women in football clubs and more than one million girls play football in Britain.

CHAPTER 9

British Writers

William Shakespeare (1564-1616)

Shakespeare was a poet and a writer of plays. His 38 plays are popular all over the world and there are translations in many languages. His plays include *Romeo and Juliet* and *Hamlet*. Shakespeare lived most of his life in Stratford-upon-Avon. Today, the town is the home of the Royal Shakespeare Company.

Charles Dickens (1812-1870)

Dickens had a hard life as a child in 19th-century London. His father was in prison for three months and his family lived there with him. When Dickens was 12 years old, he lived in a small room and worked long hours in a factory. Later, he started to write stories about these bad experiences. You can read about them in his books *David Copperfield* and *Great Expectations*.

J.K. Rowling (1965-)

J.K. Rowling was once on a long, boring train journey and started to imagine a story about a boy called Harry and a school for **wizards**. It was a great idea for a book. Five years later, she finished her first book, *Harry Potter and the Philosopher's Stone*. Sometimes, it was difficult to write because she was a **single** mother. Every day, she waited for her daughter to sleep. Then, she **typed** more of the story on her computer. Today, people all over the world love Harry Potter books and films.

CHAPTER 10

Famous Brits

A Queen with the Heart of a King

Queen Elizabeth I (1533-1603) was King Henry VIII and Anne Boleyn's daughter. She was a very influential monarch and people called her "the Queen with the heart of a King". She is important in British history because in her reign, all the other European powers respected England. But Elizabeth was sometimes cruel. She executed her cousin Mary and persecuted many Catholics.

A Strong Leader

Sir Winston Churchill (1874-1965) was Prime Minister of Britain during World War II. He was also a great writer and he received the Nobel Prize for Literature in 1953. Churchill started his **career** as a soldier in the British army. Later, he was a politician, and finally, the Prime Minister. The British people loved him because he was a strong leader, and he **didn't surrender** to Nazi Germany during World War II.

The Beatles – Four Boys from Liverpool

In the 1960s, a new pop group started with four boys from Liverpool. Their names were John, Paul, George and Ringo and the name of the group was The Beatles. Their music was very different and it was popular all over the world. Many of the songs were about love and common people on the streets of Liverpool. The Beatles stopped singing together a long time ago, but their music is still very popular today.

CHAPTERS 9-10 ACTIVITIES

1 Find six words in the puzzle. Then use them to complete the sentences.

i	n	l	f	e	b	r	r	e	f	d
k	c	e	d	a	u	g	h	t	e	r
t	r	a	j	o	u	r	n	e	y	n
h	u	d	o	z	h	c	d	s	i	g
c	e	e	r	c	r	t	a	s	r	o
n	l	r	e	c	e	i	v	e	y	w
e	f	a	c	t	o	r	y	e	i	k

1. People make cars in a ....
2. It's a long .... by train from France to Italy.
3. Sir Winston Churchill was a very strong ....
4. Queen Elizabeth II has got three sons and one ....
5. We .... e-mails from our friends every day.
6. He was very .... He killed many people.

2 Who is this famous character in a Shakespeare play? Match A to B. Then use the number and letter in each pair to find the hidden answer. The first one is done for you.

A		B
1. Winston Churchill	....	a. cousin
2. English	....	b. heart
3. Oxford	...1.....	c. prime minister
4. your father's sister's son	....	d. language
5. a part of the body	....	e. town

	a	b	c	d	e
1	P	T	(R)	A	E
2	K	S	B	O	N
3	D	I	C	X	M
4	E	U	Q	H	M
5	V	O	A	Z	G

His name is ...R...... ....

3 Complete the sentences with the people below.

A *William Shakespeare*

B *Charles Dickens*

C *J.K. Rowling*

D *Queen Elizabeth I*

E *Sir Winston Churchill*

1. .... is the writer of the Harry Potter books.
2. .... executed her cousin.
3. .... lived in Liverpool.
4. .... was a politician and a writer.
5. .... was a poet and writer of plays.
6. .... worked in a factory when he was a child.

F *The Beatles*

4 Tick (✓) the sentences true (T) or false (F).

	T	F
1. *Hamlet* is by Charles Dickens.	☐	☐
2. King Henry VIII was Queen Elizabeth II's father.	☐	☐
3. The idea for a *Harry Potter* book started on a train.	☐	☐
4. Shakespeare's father was in prison.	☐	☐
5. Churchill received a prize for literature.	☐	☐
6. Some of the Beatles' songs are about real people.	☐	☐

Did you know?

Paul McCartney is in Guinness World Records for his success as a songwriter. He has got 33 number one songs. He performed with the Beatles and with Wings, and he continues to perform today. In 1996, Queen Elizabeth II knighted him so now people call him *Sir* Paul McCartney. In 2010, he received the Gershwin Award from President Barack Obama.

CHAPTER 11

Legends and Monsters

The Lambton Worm

Five years later ...

Everyone is frightened.
There's a giant worm at the well. Every day, it comes into the town and steals our children.
Oh, no! I'm responsible for this. I didn't kill the worm five years ago, but I must kill it now!
I remember you! You didn't listen to me.
Where's the worm now?
It's at the well, but you can't kill it now. It's enormous!
I must try.
Your children are out of danger now. The worm is dead!
Hooray! Lord Lambton killed the worm!

According to Scottish legend, there's a monster in Loch Ness, a lake in Scotland. People call the monster "Nessie". In the 1930s, a tourist photographed Nessie. The photograph shows a long neck and a round head. After that, scientists used special equipment to search for Nessie. They detected big moving objects in the lake but they weren't sure what these objects were. There were many Nessie **hoaxes**, too. A man **placed** a model of Nessie in the lake and photographed it. Then, somebody placed the fossil of a big animal in the lake. However, the legend continues and tourists still search for the monster in Loch Ness today.

George and the Dragon

Many years ago, there was a **brave** knight called George. One day, he arrived at a small town. Everyone in the town was sad.

"Why is everybody sad here?" he asked.

The Princess was at the dragon's cave. George climbed onto a rock above the cave. "Don't be afraid!" he shouted. Suddenly, there was a terrible smell and the dragon appeared. "Hey, ugly dragon!" shouted George. The dragon looked at George, then George jumped on its head and killed it with his **sword**. George saved the Princess and all the young people in the town. Soon, he was a hero and a saint.

CHAPTER 12

Modern Britain

Wind Turbines

Wind turbines are an important form of energy in Britain. Britain is now planning to build a new type of turbine, with 275-metre-long wings. This mega-turbine is 600 metres above the sea, and can make electricity for over 10,000 homes.

The O2 Arena

The O2 Arena is a giant **dome** in London. The architect, Richard Rogers, designed the building to celebrate the beginning of the third millennium. It opened on 1st January, 2000 and there was a big exhibition inside. Today, the arena has got a music club, a cinema, and some bars and restaurants. Many important concerts happen there, too.

Jamie Oliver

Jamie Oliver is a famous chef. His television programmes, *The Naked Chef*, *Jamie's School Dinners* and *Jamie's Kitchen*, are very popular in Britain. Jamie's **recipes** are quick and easy to make. They're very **healthy**, too! Jamie doesn't like the unhealthy school lunches in Britain, so he's changing the school menus. Jamie also helps teenagers with problems. He teaches them how to cook and **run** a restaurant.

Mr Bean

Mr Bean is the invention of an actor, Rowan Atkinson. This funny television character lives alone in London, and his best friend is a teddy bear. Every small task, such as making a sandwich, going swimming or using a television, is difficult for him. But he always finds an unusual way to do them!

CHAPTERS 11-12 ACTIVITIES

1 Choose the correct adjective.

1. **quiet / ugly**

2. **safe / dangerous**

3. **dead / sad**

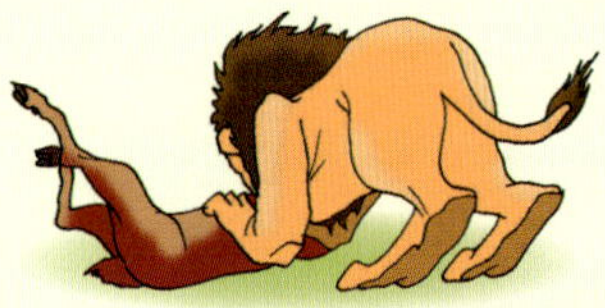

4. **expensive / hungry**

5. **round / heavy**

2 Match the parts of the sentences in A and B.

A		B
1. You can swim in a	....	a. cave.
2. Birds like eating	....	b. well.
3. Animals sometimes live in a	....	c. lake.
4. Below your head is your	....	d. worms.
5. There is water under the ground in a	....	e. neck.

Did you know?

People used the wind for power more than 2,000 years ago in Persia. Now, with the growing concern about the environment, people are again using the wind to make energy. The wind is an ideal source of energy for the UK because it's a windy country. There are small wind turbines for individual homes, as well as wind farms to generate large amounts of energy.

3 **Find six words on the worm. Circle them and use them to complete the sentences.**

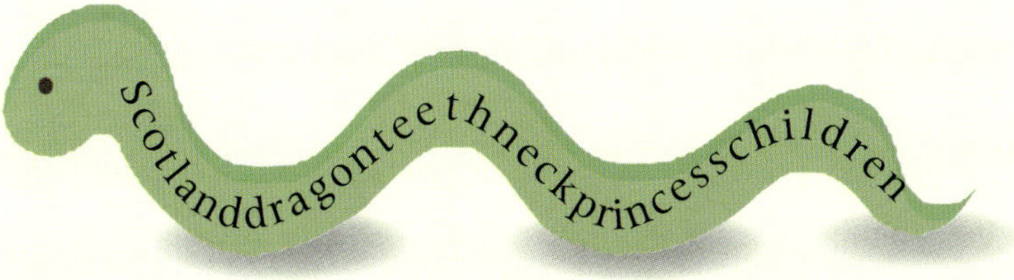

1. The Lambton Worm is unusual because it has got ....
2. The creature from the well steals ....
3. Nessie lives in ....
4. Nessie has got a long ....
5. George killed a ....
6. George saved a ....

4 **Match the sentences in A to the sentences in B.**

A

1. The British have got plans for a mega-turbine.
2. The O2 Arena is in London.
3. Jamie Oliver is a popular celebrity.
4. *The Naked Chef* is a television programme.
5. Mr Bean is a funny character.

B

.... a. He teaches teenagers with problems.
.... b. It is 600 metres above the sea.
.... c. His best friend is a teddy bear.
.... d. People go to concerts there.
.... e. Jamie Oliver makes healthy food on it.

GLOSSARY

English	Castellano	Català
bearskin	piel de oso	pell d'ós
beef	carne de ternera	carn de bou
brave	valiente	valent
buried	enterró	va enterrar
burned her at the stake	la quemaron en la hoguera	la van cremar a la foguera
career	carrera (profesional)	carrera (professional)
cellars	sótanos	soterranis
close	unido	unit
court	pista, cancha (de tenis)	pista (de tennis)
custard	natillas	natilles
daffodil	narciso	narcís
didn't surrender	no se rindió	no es va rendir
dismissed	despedida	acomiadada
dome	cúpula	cúpula
dried blood	sangre seca	sang seca
facilities	instalaciones	instal·lacions
fashion show	desfile / pase de modelos	desfilada de models
fell in love with	se enamoró de	es va enamorar de
fireworks	fuegos artificiales	focs artificials
gunpowder	pólvora	pólvora
healthy	sanas	sanes
helmet	casco	casc
hoaxes	engaños	enganys
innings	entrada	entrada
leg guards	protectores para las piernas	protector per a les cames

GLOSSARY

English	Euskara	Galego
bearskin	hartzaren larruazalarekin	pel de oso
beef	txahalki	carne de tenreira
brave	ausart	valente
buried	lurperatu zuen	enterrou
burned her at the stake	sutzarrean erre zuten	queimárona na fogueira
career	ibilbide (profesional)	carreira (profesional)
cellars	sotoak	sotos
close	lotua	unido
court	(teniseko) pista, kantxa	pista, cancha (de tenis)
custard	natilla, arrautza-esne	crema
daffodil	nartziso	narciso
didn't surrender	ez zuen amore eman, ez zen errenditu	non se rendeu
dismissed	kaleratu	despedida
dome	kupula	cúpula
dried blood	odol lehortu	sangue seco
facilities	instalazioak	instalacións
fashion show	desfile / modeloen erakustaldi	desfile / pase de modelos
fell in love with	maitemindu zen	namorouse de
fireworks	su artifizialak	fogos de artificio / artificiais
gunpowder	bolbora	pólvora
healthy	osasuntsuak	sas
helmet	kasko	casco
hoaxes	iruzurrak	enganos
innings	sarrera	entrada
leg guards	zango-babesgarriak	protectores para as pernas

GLOSSARY

English	Castellano	Català
locks	cierra	tanca
make wishes	pedir deseos	demanar desitjos
minced meat	carne picada	carn picada
noticed	se fijó en	es va fixar en
placed	colocó, puso	va col·locar, va posar
play a trick on	gastan bromas (a)	fan bromes (a)
poison	envenenar a	enverinar
pots	vasijas	atuells
pregnant	embarazada	embarassada
ravens	cuervos	corbs
recipes	recetas (de cocina)	receptes (de cuina)
rules	normas, reglas	normes, regles
run	dirigir	dirigir
search (for)	buscar; buscan	buscar; busquen
sentry box	garita de centinela	garita de sentinella
shamrock	trébol	trèvol
single	soltera	soltera
speech	discurso	discurs
sword	espada	espasa
thistle	cardo	card
tools	herramientas	eines
tournament	torneo	torneig
typed	tecleaba, escribía	teclejava, escrivia
wickets	palos (de críquet)	pals (de criquet)
wizards	magos	bruixots

GLOSSARY

English	Euskara	Galego
locks	itxi du	pecha
make wishes	desioak eskatzeko	pedir desexos
minced meat	haragi xehatu	carne picada
noticed	begiz jo zuen	reparou en
placed	ezarri zuen	colocou, puxo
play a trick on	ziria sartzen (diete), trikimailuren bat egiten (diete)	gastan brincadeiras (a)
poison	pozoitu	envelenar a
pots	ontziak	vasillas
pregnant	haurdun	embarazada
ravens	beleak	corvos
recipes	(sukaldaritzako) errezetak	receitas (de cociña)
rules	arauak	normas, regras
run	kudeatu	dirixir
search (for)	bilatzera; bila dabiltza	procurar, procuran
sentry box	zentinelaren garita	garita de sentinela
shamrock	hirusta	trevo
single	ezkongabe	solteira
speech	hitzaldi	discurso
sword	ezpata	espada
thistle	kardu	cardo
tools	lanabesak	ferramentas
tournament	torneo, txapelketa	torneo
typed	tekleatzen zuen, idazten zuen	tecleaba, escribía
wickets	(criquet-eko) hagak, mastak	paus (de críquet)
wizards	aztiak	magos

A United Nation

Great Britain, the United Kingdom, the British Isles … are they the same or different? Read the following and find out.

GREAT BRITAIN

In 1282, England's King Edward I conquered Wales and then he was their king too. In 1603, King James VI **united** England and Scotland and decided to call his new kingdom Great Britain. But Great Britain wasn't officially a country until 1707.

THE UNITED KINGDOM

In 1801, Ireland **joined** Great Britain and these countries together formed the United Kingdom. But many Irish people in the south weren't happy about this. They wanted their own country. So, in 1922, the people in the south formed their own country, the Republic of Ireland, and the people in the north of Ireland stayed with Great Britain. This is why the UK is now the United Kingdom of Great Britain and Northern Ireland.

united	unió, unificó	va unir, va unificar	bateratu zuen, batu zuen	uniu, unificou
joined	se unió a	es va unir a	-ekin bat egin zuen	uniuse a

THE BRITISH ISLES

The British Isles includes Great Britain, Northern Ireland, the Republic of Ireland and over 6,000 small islands.

1 Circle the correct letter to answer true (T) or false (F). Then write the circled letters to complete the sentence below.

	T	F
1. King Edward I was the king of England and Wales.	p	n
2. Great Britain consists of three islands.	a	o
3. Many people from southern Ireland didn't want to join Great Britain.	u	i
4. People in the north of Ireland remained a part of the Republic of Ireland.	o	n
5. More than 6,000 islands are a part of the British Isles.	d	n

The British don't use the euro. They've got the _ _ _ _ _ .

2 What is it?

1. The United Kingdom + The Republic of Ireland + Many small islands = ...
2. England + Scotland + Wales = ...
3. Great Britain + Northern Ireland = ...

FLAGS

Richard I introduced the red cross of St George as the national flag of England in 1194.

The Scottish flag with the St Andrew's cross first appeared in 1512.

King James VI of Scotland was also the King of England and he wanted a flag for the new Great Britain. In 1606, the individual flags of England and Scotland together formed the first Union Flag. In 1707, Queen Anne decided to make it the official national flag of Great Britain.

When Great Britain and Ireland joined together in 1801, they needed a flag to represent Ireland too, so they created the Union Jack.

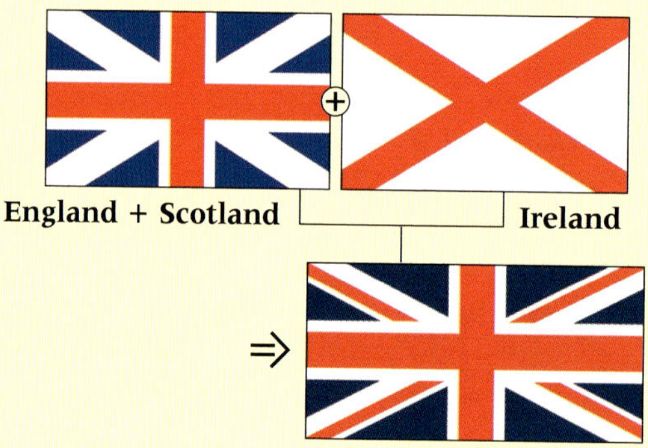

Although the St Patrick's cross wasn't the official flag of Ireland, it was a symbol of Ireland, and so they included it in the Union Jack.

The Union Jack is a combination of the crosses of St George, St Andrew and St Patrick. The flag of Wales doesn't appear on the Union Jack. This is because Wales was a province of England from the 13th century, not a kingdom.

3 Which countries do the sentences refer to? Tick (✓) the correct column(s).

	Wales	England	Scotland	Ireland
1. The Union Jack includes the flags of these countries.				
2. This country's flag was blue and white.				
3. The cross of St Patrick represented this country.				
4. King James VI was their king.				
5. Their flags formed the first Union Flag.				
6. It was a province, not a kingdom.				

4 When did it happen? Match the dates to the sentences.

1194 1512 1606 1707 1801

.... 1. The British created today's Union Jack.

.... 2. King James VI created the first Union Flag.

.... 3. Queen Anne decided to make the first Union Flag the country's official flag.

.... 4. The St Andrew's cross first appeared on the Scottish flag.

.... 5. Richard I introduced the Red Cross of St George as the national flag of England.

MINI TASK

Look on the Internet or in an encyclopedia for information about the symbols representing Wales. Write a few sentences about these symbols.